I0224750

still.

by

Corey Ruzicano

Finishing Line Press
Georgetown, Kentucky

still.

ACKNOWLEDGMENTS

Lisa Hubbell, Hannah Ojendyk, Gina Hubbell, the Suh family, Tonasia Jones,
Claudia Rankine, Caroline Chu, Fanta Ballo, Fin Kruckemeyer, LeeAnn
Dowd, Zoe Westbrook, James Kennedy, Jack Babnew, Andrea Hiebler, Lynette
D'Amico, Dr. P Carl, Lauren Cortizo, Gabe Gibbs, Garrett Kim, Allie Gibbs,
Victor Cervantes Jr, Edward Kimszal, and Reverend Hamilton.

Publisher: Leah Huete de Maines
Editor: Christen Kincaid
Cover Art: Caroline Chu
Illustrations: Lisa Hubbell, Edward Kimszal, & Corey Ruzicano
Author Photo: Zack Arch
Cover Design: Elizabeth Maines McCleavy

Order online: www.finishinglinepress.com
also available on amazon.com

Author inquiries and mail orders:
Finishing Line Press
P. O. Box 1626
Georgetown, Kentucky 40324
U. S. A.

{what's inside}

for the courage givers
and theirs.

"To love. To be loved. To never forget your own insignificance. To never get used to the unspeakable violence and the vulgar disparity of life around you. To seek joy in the saddest places. To pursue beauty to its lair. To never simplify what is complicated or complicate what is simple. To respect strength, never power. **Above all, to watch. To try and understand.** To never look away. And never, never to forget."

—Arundhati Roy, *The Cost of Living*

before.

the day before we drove to the canyon
the air seemed alive with promise
      a desert like that is so dry it generates static electricity
          my brother tells me on minute twenty-three
              of the longest phone call we've ever had
              the one where he tells me (aloud)
              he doesn't know
              if he'll ever really change
              if he'll ever be different than he is right now.
              he tells me,
    out here you can shock someone with the slightest touch

the day before we drove to the canyon
we drank instant coffee
and warmed tortillas on the stove top
and told each other things we hadn't before
the day before we drove to the canyon
i was someone else.

         there on the edge
looking at the people
looking down into the canyon
looking at the ridges on either side of all that nothing

the boy in the blue striped shirt
tells his mother
with tangential authority
      if you tripped right here,
      you could tumble
      all the way
      and all the way
      is a whole mile down

i am amazed that he can imagine a mile
        that at 27 i cannot conceive of how long a mile really is
              can still only conceive of the few inches in front of my feet

someone-else's grandfather cocks his head to one side
and tells this someone-else's grandson
and you know how long it'd take ya to get to the bottom?
all the way till your next birthday.

i look out into all that opposite-of-something
and recognize myself
more in all this nothing
than in any other something
more than a mirror:
all this air on the way to being

i think of that fall
into the canyon
in and out of years
and time bending like space
       of which at 27 i am less able to conceive than i was as a boy in blue stripes
       and somehow still
       can
   imagine
if played in reverse
all of life might look something like that
one tumble into the next
traceably linear
in retrospect alone.

dizzy with the height
and the wonder
i look out
and am different
in a way you wouldn't see through the tape of that fall
no different from one frame
and the next
no different at all
       except the expansion
       of the space between
       every
       single
       atom

i look out
at everything that canyon holds
and does not
and i thought i knew what grand meant
but it turns out i was wrong.

fall

water's falling in the domestic terminal
of the san francisco airport
after missing the flight
after running all the way
after all the inching traffic
the traveler next to me
politely ignores
the very human sounds
being made beside him
  the excess of salt water
  and hiccuped breath
and reads
the theory of poker
and i think
how tired i am
of thinking about
winning
or losing

outside the window another plane
takes off
i watch
all those lives
for a moment
going in exactly the same direction.

san francisco is already a poem
candlestick park
oyster point
land's end
  green is gone
  grey is going
  i could no longer hold my tongue
  september does it to me
  every year

summer is past
  it is time for telling true things
  and burying hatchets
 if you have them

i carry the weight
in the sweetness of summer
i hide easy in all that freedom
i hold the vinegar on my tongue
cut it thick with sugar
and lemon
swallow it back
with the rest of the secrets
it all goes down smooth in june
carefree and wild with the long afternoons
sliding syrup into evening
the sky so steeped with sun
we drink it all night long
throw up hands
in the warm wind
          and panic when it turns and falls
          with september
          the panic of all this weight
          of cold coming in
          bitter across the american west
          the panic
          of suddenly
          finally
          setting down this load
            this good, good ache of you
          of knees buckling
          of finally having to own up
          to being unable to carry this
          any further.

we had one magic hour,
my sweet friend,
where things sat still for us
where we could keep each other warm

where our dotted lines intersected with softness
but one hour
        even one magic hour
is still only one hour
which is to say
one magic hour
is not enough
which is to say
suddenly
finally
i understand
        and every light in the world goes out.

the leaves turn to mulch beneath our feet
i have mourned enough;
this hatchet heart is heavy,
it is time to put it down.

song triptych: this is how you make me feel

1.

like the spaces between my ribs are expanding
and filling with light

like the window's down and the spring air
is soft against my face as we drive over the hills
from wild cat canyon to happy valley
by every lonely cow
       lonely only to me
       as the observer
       but entirely content
       each within themselves

like moving across vast black skies
through that somehow-ever-expanding darkness that is
the outer
space
losing pieces
gathering heat
growing leaner with flight

like gradual
hard-earned
understanding

2.

like red engines hissing
over the tracks
like crowds of set jaws
like you have something for me
you with the grit in your grin
you, who put the led in my marrow
       fire in my fists
       violet bright against the dying night

you with the heavy boots
you with the painted arms
you with the hurt hardened silver tongue

you are palms meeting at dusk
you are shadows growing on the wall
you are steam coming off the sidewalks
you are the glimmer
that this might be it
        and this might be
        it

this is how you make me feel:
like there is only one option left
and of course it doesn't look
like i thought it would
but that's the trick of the living
and it's all we can do
just to get free:
come together
right now
together we'll be
a place worth being

3.

like late gold burning off into
bruise purple july nights
long and hot and slow
passing the joint around the stoop
a film of salt on every cheek
spreading over every close-mouthed smile
cracked open in that
accepting kind of ache
all of us piled on top of each other
sharing our blocks
with soot and rats
and tinny distant bodega radio
and sureness

that none of what you say
will stay true for long
will melt like this mango paleta
that i have no business writing about
leaving only cavities
and sticky fingers in its wake
but god i'm weak
and god we've got summer now
and god the way your crooked smile
pulls on me
i can't seem to do anything
but reach
for another hit

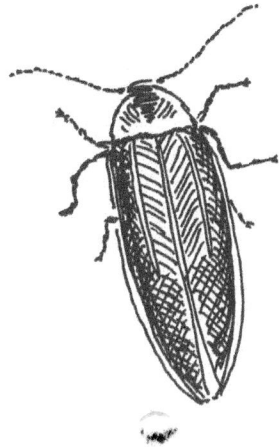

5660 college avenue.

when i think of home
    i still think of the bend in the tracks
        as the train leaves the station at rockridge
            where i look out across the tops of all the houses
                the kingdom of red roofs and redwoods
                    in the direction of that uncanny palm tree
                      the sentinel of your childhood home.

      i think of the black and white checkerboard kitchen floor
           and on it, your mother's socked feet
              minding the stock and forgiving my misshapen matzo balls
i think of sitting on the floor next to your chair while you play poker
      of you holding my constantcold feet in your everwarm hands
    of your patchwork family sewn of friend and blood and song
  of the avocado tree in your backyard
      and the view from that west-facing window
           the one i always felt like i was looking in,
                    though i was looking out.

i admit:
i made up that detail about your mom's socked feet.
i do not know what she wears on her feet in the kitchen
or out to get the paper
or if she goes out to get the paper at all.
while these pictures loom so large in my head
i caught most of them only through stolen sideways glances,
      too afraid to look anything in the eye
      most of all, you.
and yet, when i think of home
you are what i think of
it's harder to chart than i'd ever have guessed
what collects in this life
what does not fade
i've lived 9,689 days on this planet and

i marvel: most of them
pass through the hourglass without anything sticking
while these few stubborn grains stay stuck
pull me back again and again
whole worlds in these moments that whole years of this life cannot stand up to
and how strange that math is.

my whole life long i will wonder why
i couldn't answer
when you called my name.

cobweb dispatch.
after Nikki Giovanni

i can admit
it is a strange place for a web
this old amsterdam apartment
with many more rooms than people
the ceilings much higher
than most
ground dwellers
are willing
or able
to climb
and yet i am rarely
lonely

there was the year
where an army of yellow jackets
took roost in the walls
some of their mustard shelled corpses
still lay curling in corners
the few that evaded the vacuum
if not the gas
but even so
my work is not
much of a match
for soldiers like those
militant
and born of fury
charging through my carefully woven
world
no
even that season
was not
the abundance
one might have imagined it to be

once a platoon of ants
sent scores of scouts
beaten back

for only so long
until all
had to be eradicated
sending poisoned spoils back to the queen
killing the hill
at the heart

a hornet the size of a walnut
once woke me from my reverie
i am startled
and then bemused
realizing how silly we are
thinking we can keep
the earth outside

there is a girl beneath
the silk chandelier
wrapping herself in color
there is a girl
talking to the empty room
there is a girl
laying on the floor
trying to become

and still
here
i stay
it is a lean life
but a quiet one
no one to distrust
which i value now
in this wild
sleepless
city
i spin my
webs
i feed myself
i do what i can
and do not wonder

why anyone
should fear
someone
so
small.

when in doubt

the heart is a muscle
the opposite of instinct
like most things
in this life
its beating its loving
in equal measure
its beating its living
a violence from within
this life was a fight

einstein and bohr
wrote letters to each other
the great interpreters
of our universe's existence
then and now
argued like hearts
stitched together a love over
34 years of doubt
discovery
takes that
closeness requires
distance
everything
needs
what we imagine
it could not stand
and yet
nothing rests
certainty
is not a place
we ever reach
only something
we forever reach toward
god does not throw dice
einstein would warn
and still
we have no maps to show for it

no bow to tie around
the ever expanding puzzle
of quantum mechanics
even after years of study
einstein,
bohr would chide
don't tell god what to do
and around and around
sending back new ways
to tease out reason
poking holes in each other's work
as an offering
figure this
einstein would say
imagine a box of light
still
there are more shots to take
still
there are more questions
because thank god
there will always be
more questions

        we lay
        we two
        in the deafening quiet
        of this answerless night
        his breath on my back
        his mouth on the blade of me

when bohr died
someone photographed
the blackboard in his office
and there
even to his last breath
the plans for *the box of light*
even to his last breath
all these questions
with a heart so full of love

and so full of doubt

here in the dark
this fist
this rose
this beating in his chest
was the difference between him
and not
him
was the space between
the answer
and the question

and i want science
want numbers
want proofs
want something more than words
to tell him:

kid truth,
roll the stone away
i know they stole from you
pillaged and took
but what did they get
when you're all you have
you're still worth every penny
i tossed in this well
every candle i lit
every word on the blackboard
every prayer in the night
for even a scrap
of that heart

god doesn't throw dice
einstein wrote
but even in all that bluster
he could never be sure
only ever
was he sure

of his heart
when he wrote to bohr
after the boats in bottles
all sunk
after the paper airplanes
all went down
not long before the end
     not often in this life
     has a human being caused me
     such joy by his mere presence
     as you did

          hey kid,
          i'm never sure of anything
          but looking at you
          i can hear the sound
          that light would make
          if it sung
          looking at you
          the question
          fills my heart
          more than the answer
          ever could.

marathon.

The Day The Bomb Went Off on boylston street
midstride of the boston marathon
was not the day i thought the world was ending.

i come up the stairs from the basement theater
and see the hoards of
scattered people
the lost service
the cacophony of
not yet knowing what
but knowing
somehow
Something Big has happened
the instants trying to account for who should be accounted for
       the immediate list-making in the hurricane's eye
       the only kind of order i am any good at
we are ushered inside
       or we must have been,
       though i don't remember how
       or by whom
i sign stranded friends into my dorm
clear off the extra-long twin
to make room for the extra loved ones
       not yet the extra-loved one
       whom i wouldn't hole up with until
       three days into lockdown

       that first day comes back only in snatches of
       big eyed thick-aired calm
       the moments of not believing
       but i was always good at days like that
       crisis narrows your options
       i was always better
       with fewer options

not two days before
in the dark spring evening

in the doorway of
what was then
sweetwater tavern
i had told him
no
we shouldn't
{even though
i do
feel it
something unnamable
but tell the (extra-loved) boy something else
       the boy who would
       next october
       turn up to visit out of the blue
       wearing the la dodgers cap
       i'd mailed him
       on a july whim
       and three sheets to the wind
       ask me to marry him
              when i tell that story
              i say *i laugh at him*
              and tell him he's too drunk
              i do not say
              what was true
              which was that
              of course
              i pictured it
              which was exactly why
              of course
              i let him fall asleep in my arms
              in the stranger's cambridge apartment
              and
              of course
              sneak out the window with the rising sun
              as soon as he empties himself
              into the rhythm of soft breath}

The Day We Make A Break For It
and walk to mass general hospital

to give blood
we walk through the common
which is now stunningly studded
with g.i. joe lookalikes
strapped with all kinds
of killing instruments
and i say to my roommate
someone yell cut already
because it feels more possible
that we've somehow ended up on set of some
high budget action movie
than our park being lined with military brigade
on the look out for a boy our age
and his brother

The Third Day Of Lockdown
i am trying
to make myself useful
in a one bedroom apartment
playing nurse to injured friends
with this boy my age
only two-days-ago-spurned
      who could
      in another life have been instead
      my boy, this age
we clamber over each other
and all our close-mouthed questions
improvising pain remedies
and meditation techniques
for those who had actually
been present
at the blast
      the air gauzy with all the secrets we had spilled
      with the kiss stolen
      the hands pressed against chests
      the wrenching apart of bodies
      the *shouldn't*
      the knowing
      this was not

a Good Idea
and i was all about
Good Ideas
back then
or at the very least
pretending to be
leaning over the injured body
of the very girl
i told him
was the reason
we *shouldn't*

      which was
      yet another lie
      she was only
      a convenient
      reason
      to point to
      instead of the
      Capital-G Good Reason
      not to go on and adore him
      which i hadn't yet
      courage or conviction enough
      to name
there we were
our hands empty
armed with nothing but silence
to treat her shellshock

The Day They Caught Him
it turns out
was
The Day I Thought The World Was Ending
the day they caught him
or rather
the night
      because i remember it
      as shouts
      bright and ruthless
      wolf like

        against the dark
he was found
hiding in an overturned boat
in a backyard in watertown
white boys
pour over
over the common
the public garden
in droves
beating their shirtless torsos
swinging
like released fugitives
like primates
from the columns of the gazebo
shouting victory
like schoolboys
pretending to have won
        like the killing of one boy
        could be The Answer

and i know
i must be crazy
not to want
the surefire answer
of his end
but all i can think of
is the boy
in the boat
        how afraid he must have been
all i can think of
is the boy
and the lives that boy
was able to take
wanted to take
        how afraid he must have been
and still
not yet old enough to drink
and still
when is old enough to know

when is old enough to be held responsible
when is evil, *evil*
and not the product of other things
and how can i even wonder these things
when there are
at the hands of this boy
and his brother
lives
    lost
        and losing
        how afraid they must have been
        how afraid we're asked to be
        how afraid we all are

i watch
these boys
crying victory
with their teeth
on the common
and the heat rises up
pricks at the back of my neck
my throat
constricts
i turn tail
and go back
to my dorm room
alone
        no boys
        loved or otherwise
and sit
my back against the door
my thighs
pressed into the off white
linoleum tiles
        that i remember as off white linoleum tiles
        though they very well were something else entirely
and thought
days ago
we had seen the worst of it
and it turns out we were wrong.

to you before i knew—

there are more telescopes in touscan than anywhere else in the world.
when i'm thinking about Mosts, and sometimes i am, i think about that.
and these states, these things i don't know—
michigan makes the Most breakfast cereal
louisiana's got the Most crayfish
west virginia with marbles and hawaii with macadamia nuts.
these are things i didn't know before i looked to tell you;
i wonder what i'll remember.
what i won't forget—
that there's a city in colorado called loveland,
        where thousands of valentines are re-mailed each year
that the world's smallest park is in portland,
        made for leprechauns and snail races.
that elvis had a doorbell under his dining room table in graceland
that volcanoes made hawaii
that tom sawyer painted fences in missouri
that dorothy wasn't in kansas anymore

there are places that you've never seen
there are people that you haven't been
it's true
but the things that you know
and the you that you are
is more than the peaches in georgia
more than the golden gate
more than the arkansas diamonds
or the teeth on the gators florida
you're truer blue than the big sky state
a bigger lone star than texas
more at liberty than the statue or the bell.

i don't know much about Mosts or Firsts or Lasts.

i don't know which states you've been to
i don't know all the stories you know
but the ones that you've given me,
the things that you've taught

leave my world larger than it was before.
you are these united states
as full and as fraught and as filled with fault lines and promise and fear
and histories,
forgotten and remembered,
big and small

and no one knows all of it
there is never enough time
to come home to all of it.
but you teach me to treasure the places i do.
i suppose we learn to accept that
as more than enough.

say when

when the moon was a thumbnail
and the sky was still paint
i loved you
still and blue and dark against my own palms
heavy in the safe house of my throat
i choked on all the unuttered letters.
i learned.

when the moon was a coin
and the land was still page
i loved you
static over song
lightning pop of sunshine soda
a rumble overhead
a sky cracked open
a sudden happening—
for a moment
i held
some new Everything
and then Nothing.
i learned.

when the moon was a bone
and the night was still kind
i loved you
sharp edged and secret
in the smooth stone stream
jagged and graceless
eyes adjusting
not-quick-enough
to the dusk everywhere descending.
i ran before the dust could settle
i learned.

when the moon was plate
and the days had grown short
i loved you

like a pillar of salt
like sneakers slung over the telephone line
something built to move
frozen in place
i retire my voice
for a season
i learned.

when the moon was a pearl
and the sun was
the sun
i loved you.
and love you
and stumble
and stew
and struggle
and stay
and continue to
love you.
and learn.

remember
the moon
is only a mirror;
she shines
because you do.

what words there weren't

1.

a buzzing
every word
every whisper
a world i had not chosen
and it frightened me
it heavied me like lead

2.

the spinning
spokes
of a beached bicycle
a whirring reminder
of how soon things are lost

      this is what i have of yours
      of you
      everything i can remember
      it's funny what it adds up to
      the paper doll you
      instead of the you that breathes
      and laughs and grinds your teeth in sleep
      what i do and do not know
      this is what i have
      this is what i gave them
      what i try to give them still

3.

warm wood underfoot
an old sad song
roofs and rain falling on them
lightning bugs

the smell of the air in your home town
magic pieces of the world that
no matter how many times they're named
can never
need never
fully be explained

       i realize
       as i try to describe my mother
       that i would never have enough words for it
       that every writer
       since the first
       had been trying to put into something that would stand
       how it feels to love someone so much
       there will never be enough words for it
       that this life
              so infinitely filled with two sided coins
would never have enough stories or pictures or music enough to make someone
understand how terribly, how entirely, how much bigger and truer and more real
than any binding law or physical compound, i loved my mother.
and the tears of that love,
the salt of all of it would dry
unseen on this paper and the only sliver of silver in all this is the thought that
someday someone might read this and know that they too love their mother
in some implacable way
different and the same
no more or less true than the way i love mine.

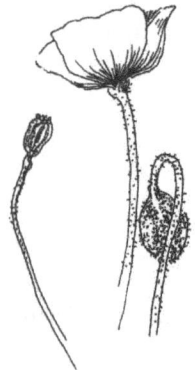

on what it might be like to freeze to death.

by looking at the molecules,
you change them
he says
voice postured
with thick-throated dignity
his hand on my neck
your perception creates reality.

i go cold
i lose my grip
all i can feel is the mud in my veins
starting to collect and get heavy—
    move
        says the hair on the back of my neck
    run
        swells the skin under my nails
    chew your way out if you have to
        hammers the morse code of my pulse
    things are slowing down
    people freeze to death like this
    you have frozen
        will freeze to death like this

throat closes
tongue swells
something wide-eyed and feral
stirs in the sediment of my spine
i look for my bones
    for words
    for some kind of solid self within me
my head swims
      what do i remember?
        where do i exist?
          how can i fix my molecules from changing under his gaze?
            what of my self did i leave on the island?
              what can i hold
                because it can no longer be my breath

perceptions creates reality
i spit splinters

for him
       and hims before him
i have shuttled between
believing myself
                 and an agnostic static
                    where my story should be

courageless clutching at facts
                and moorless unsure-ness

voiding my body altogether
       living somewhere between
              zipping myself into the valley of purgatory
                  watching the flashes of my life
                      like strips of film i both do and do not
                    recognize

i watch the door to my self
grow like alice
the handle foreboding, the threshold immense
my arms too weak, my hands unsteady
my keys somewhere in the bottom of my bag
time seems to suspend
as i watch the fork in the road for signs of life
trying to make out what survival might look like—

      the soft snow drift of staying
        still

             or the scrape
                the scrap
                   the scratching out of
                       into
                       away
          something snaps

perception creates reality
        on that
                alone
                    he and i
                            can agree
and his
won't write mine any longer.

on the hike to church's blue hole

reverend hamilton leads me down the dirt path
the island heat limitless
the sky impossibly blue
and everything else suddenly the same
he tells me the story of each thing growing
as far as we can see
his eyes
and mine

this
this is ironwood
he says
pointing to a tree dotted in papery lilac blooms,
its wood is so dense it will not float
not even in seawater
and it grows so slowly
some live to be a thousand years or more
this
the seagrape tree
we love to eat the jam of the seagrapes
and the seagrape tree loves dry salty soil
so we are a perfect pair
he laughs
the wide wick of his hands turning the page of each leaf
each a large sheath of redgreen wax
this
the cinnia pod, favorite of the sheep and goats
this
the moringa tree
the miracle tree
pointing out its arms open wide in greeting
boasting bright white victory blooms in her hair
we eat every part of this tree
the blossoms, the leaves, the bark

reverend hamilton knows every face
every name
on this island

there is not a soul we pass
that does not raise a hand in brightened greeting
at us both:
the reverend and the interloper
this
rock bush
you chew its leaves
        bitter and dark
to cure the sore throat
this
pond bush
boil and drink
to cure back pain
this
the ginny bush
you burn this,
        a blushing blossom
        tiny in his vast palm
and it will keep the sand flies away
this
the seven year apple tree
this
the rams horn
this
the spider lily
        each name a story
        each story a life
this
we call dogwood fishpoison tree
        he says
        as we walk along the shoreline
        i cling to each syllable
        praying i lose not a single one
the plant is poison to fish
in fact,
the fishermen take the essence from the bark
and wave it near the fish to put them to sleep
and they swim in circles and you can catch them with your bare hands
it is not poison to us

we use it to take away aches in the head or teeth
and to treat nervousness or trouble sleeping
this
love weed
> reaching down for what looks like spools and spools of orange
> twine

legend has it
you roll it up in a ball in one hand
and say aloud the name of the boy or girl you would like to love
for life
and throw it into a tree
if the vine catches
you will have your love

and if not?
> i ask
> he laughs
> a deeper warm than the sun on our faces

if not we boil this plant into a tea and drink it
better than viagra
> he jokes.

this
silver top palm
deceptively strong
this is how we make our roof
our baskets
hat
fan
bag
this
poisonwood
> he says
> i draw back my hand

if you get the milk of this on your skin
it will make you itch
but it produces a dark red berry
that the white crowned pigeon loves
and we love the white crowned pigeon on this island.

sometimes we know only what something is not right for
not yet knowing that it has an exact and necessary purpose.

how did we get so far from you, mother,
green living ancestor of us all?
how did i get so far from myself?
i wish i could chart
and know
the balms of my own body
this clearly.
i pray
for the first time
in a long time
palms pressed
head bowed
in some half performance of
piety
begging for the lessons of
mourning
a way of life that is no longer
or perhaps never was
a way that admires without any need of ownership
please
let us learn to care
so we have the chance to learn
each and every
exact and necessary purpose.
please
give me the strength to care
even alone.
there are answers
in every molecule
please
teach me to listen again
so i can understand
the answers
before we've killed them.

sleepless notes

1.
waiting heart in throat
tight-fisted listening
through the walls every time he leaves the room
praising the flush of the pipes
the squeak of the faucet
like a homily
the symphony of routine
                    routine rage to cover the ache
                constant clench everywhere
            staying up the nights with his hurt
        while the rest of him sleeps
        eyes
    face
aching to close like the soft flower i fight not to be
but always am anyway
and still
staying open
learning to cry so silent and still it's as if you aren't
learning to cry so silent and still
the drop of each tear on the sheet
is the loudest bullet in your gun
feeling ridiculous
        for trying to make things better with
                a lemon popsicle,
                a fresh coat of paint,
        for trying to make beautiful
        things that were not
feeling ridiculous
and still
        trying to make beautiful
                things that are not.

2.

you're not as easy to get as you think you are
he tells me

and i'm not sure what to say
i am trying everything i can think of
to get got
i think
but don't say
which is perhaps the problem
somewhere in india the doctors pull 527 teeth from a boy's mouth
like so many unshelled seeds
                bullets
                pearls

he looks at me like dark water
        and don't get me wrong
        i have long since mistaken myself
        for someone easily understandable
        have long been
        a word pulled from
        paper
        unpronounceable
        have long numbed to the dentist's drill
        trying to carve out a path
        to all that rot
somehow
still
it stings

shoreless
i wade
sure shouldered
into your memories with you
scraps of sound from the field
something shelled under our feet
i'm testing a theory
he says
when i sleep alone
he says
i don't dream about her
he says
but when i sleep next to you

he says
i do

and i don't know what to say
because i never know what to say
so i say *i'm sorry*
the tongue i am
fluent in
the pebbles i throw at your window
and let the rest of me turn
cold quicksand
into myself
paint the inside of his wrist
with the tips of my fingers
back and forth
until he drifts into dreams of her
and marvel
at how many things
       could accumulate between us
       in less than the time it takes
       to crack an egg
at how we were white and yolk one
       and within the space of that crack
       now entirely separated out
       in different shells altogether
at how her name dries the marrow from my bones
       that now i am filled with echoes instead of iron

i muscle out my lungs
waiting for the catch
of a true deep breath
that doesn't come
everything in me water
flowing to the lowest point
sucked to the drain of something lower than i could ever have known
existed
my ribs closing in
every breath fighting
the cartoon reality

of every wall of this body collapsing in on itself

i have tried to make a home in this doubt
for too long
lingered long enough in the doorway of sureness
to know it would not have me
waited blind in the eye of this question
and still
527 teeth and each holding tighter to each new secret than the last
527 teeth and still not enough to choke this down
527 teeth and still no right words to say
because what words can say *please live*
besides
please
live

i catch and hold fast
even with all those barbs in my palms
i sit up with all his hurt
she sings to me all night
while he dreams
tomorrow
when he asks why i'm so tired
i'll shrug silent smile
and think of the late nights in the dark
squeezing each other's hand
sending morse code across the chasm of the cab
whispering *here*
into the tin can at the end of the string
the one i keep pressed to my ear
so hard i can hear
the ocean
between us
and wish
with every starfish
i had more than shells and string
to hold you

3.

i'm pretending i don't exist for a minute
i tell him
like if i could lay still enough
i could survive it for us both
but what i mean is
i exist and i can barely stand it
cannot stand it
and so am making myself smaller
to fit inside of it
so i am not always running over
because the size that i am is wrong
the size that i love you is wrong
the size of my palms is wrong
but i am here on earth
and what can i do

i begin to say the opposite of things i mean
why do we have to talk about it
i say
i don't care
i say
because i was raised by wolves
i say
because i am wolf and i raised myself
i say
because i am wild and don't know how to
unwild myself small enough to fit inside of this life

i try to explain myself
and the words just come out wrong
every time with you
the words do not fit
i cannot make myself the right size
to be big enough to say what i mean

he asks me to sing
and i do

28 teeth and i
whisper
elton john
against the darkness
and his quiet breathing
and his hands in my hair

i drift and then wake
and wait
for the color to come back across the world
i look out the window
for the lighted sky alone
and all want to say is
please be here when i get back
please be here
with your strong hands
and your heavy heart
i promise
if my words are not
my arms will be strong enough
to hold it
here.

more—

That Night i stood
on the armrest between the driver and the passenger seats
between the freckled arms of friends
stretching my spine up out of the moon roof
arms valley wide and alive
flying through the fog and the redwoods and the smell of eucalyptus and life
for once i was nowhere else but there on that dark road stretching on into
infinite.

That Night we spent putting out matches with our fingertips
knowing faith for once
knowing
if you do it quick enough
if you hold it long enough
you can put fire to sleep with your skin.

That Night you sat beside me on the worn jersey sheets
quietly
not touching
or asking questions
or trying to do anything at all
but stand sentinel
while i slept for two and a half hours
the first two and a half hours in three days

That Night we sat on the swings
of that deserted playground in chinatown at 2 am
and you let me read you several passages of the bell jar
and letters to a young poet
and infinite jest
and whatever pretentious dreaming
i could get my hands on
dizzy and alive
with the whisper of *somedays*
we
the living needles
revolving on the old 45

scratching away
at surviving
itching at understanding
at all these questions
wild alive
with want.

not enough people write poems about the good friends.
these are the great loves
not the match
or the flame
but the skin between.

they are the way to keep going
when wayward
the soft ground beneath the flint
the ash you rise from again and again.

for That Night
and That
and all the rest
                    are the reason to keep on.

south orange to penn station.

the sky burning persimmon
over a grey jersey goodbye
flying kites against the world turning
faster than we could see it
i had made myself a liar again
and try to catch The Truth in my shaking hands
never able to hold the solid stone i imagine it to be
you cannot convince someone to love you
i trace the letters over my palm
again
again
i know it
have known it and somehow still need the reminding
i have only ever wanted to, once before
have only ever ached like this once
       but it lasted eleven years
      so you do the math
           and here i was lying again
           all this *just once in my life* nonsense
           i had never wanted anything ever just once in my life
           i had wanted over and over
           overlapping wanting and
               wanting
          and recoiling
       and wanting more
    and again
  and anyway
so long as i didn't have to admit it
you cannot fix anything for anyone
but how could that be when it was all i'd ever done
          aside from the wanting
and was that what my love meant
when i tried it on as a verb

he was a hurt i still couldn't solve
a puzzle still jagged and scattered over the table
splintered across the floor

in the shards of light that shuddered
through the bare branches above
he was everywhere
the space around everything
but he himself
nothing
never there

the first decade
of the new millennia is closing
and i am up
with the ghosts
trespassing on these hours of theirs
my head in my grandfather's hands
holding them
frame after frame
as he sleeps into nothing
slipping quietly from life into death
holding
the hand i now know well
the hand whose severed fingers
i have twice picked from the sawdust of our garage
and watched the doctor reattach with needle and thread
the hand
with a split down one thumb
from that same saw
the same sew
the same seam
the same hand
with a workman's grasp caked in
every crease worn down
every scar finally soft

at the end
i was surprised
to find his hands
still holding onto mine
or rather
holding *still* onto mine
mine which were

for once
steady
quiet
seam to seam
in the eye of the storm
at ease
in the heart of chaos

he was not a man i had spent much of this life loving
quiet and distant
but even now
i can't help but feel
that his life
however small
and creased
and not known
deserved some redemption
        or perhaps just hope
        in vain
        that all lives do

i watch the boys around me
trying on every day what it is to be a man
trying to be both Good and Man at once
trying to become
which so often felt punctuated and propelled by
the legacy of leaving
wondering
when any of us will understand what strong really is
or rather
what really is strong
what the measure of metal is
what metal miracles take
[all] i['ve ever] want[ed was] to close the wound
my arms are open
but that means they are also empty
and so i am taking up with ghosts
and liars
again

this great grief
the one we all had
just from living
that felt so personal
and specific
and awake
and was
in fact
the most universal
and mundane,
the most every day
we were all all bad
and all all good
and all all innocent of what was coming
we were all still packing our backpacks
and running away from home
we were all afraid of who we really were
we were all staring at the sun
        blinding ourselves over and over
        just to survive
        just to keep beginning in this world of endings
we were all peaches
        all dying as we ripened
we were all
we were all

and there was nothing for it.
just the hands
split
and creased
and empty
and open
and there.

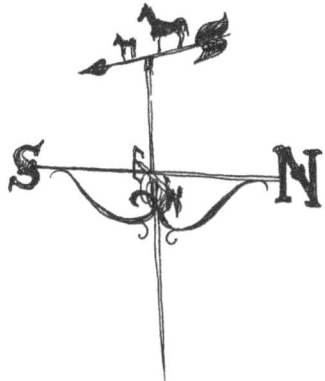

next door

there's some version of this story
where i learn to drive at 16
where i never make a practice of sitting outside myself
wondering when i will start moving
in time
with everyone else

there's some version of this story
where i stay the firecracker
i was born into
where i still say *blue jay*
before any other word
and never bother to say anything less wild
where my river rolls right on into the sea
where i meet no fork in the road
and pick the lane marked SILENT

there's some version of this story
where i never give the quiet up
where i marry a handyman
in a small town where i teach english
and can peaches
and live small
and ask my questions only to my
pages at night

there's some version of this story
where i wear only black
and hop the first tour bus
the summer after the first time he touches me
and live late nights
carrying equipment
and drinking whiskey
       or learning to like whiskey
            or who gives a shit if you like it
                 in this life i drink whiskey
and live in my nerves

there's some version of this story
where i tell everyone the truth
where i pay the price sooner
where what you see
is what you get

maybe there's another version of this story
this one that is my life
where i never meet you
where you don't hang my coat up for me in that sardined village dive bar
where i never lose my heart to you
maybe
very likely
there's another version of this story
where we don't feel like two kids on the run
maybe
almost certainly
there are infinite versions of this story
without the two of us
ever in it together
        even in this one
        we were rarely *really* together
maybe
there's another version of this story
where we tell the truth
        at least to each other
and shame the devil
but it isn't this one
there's some version of this story
where i realize you don't belong
in it, earlier
where i learn to drive at 16
and drive towards myself
but it's not this one.
in this one
it takes longer.
in this one
i am 28 and still
in the passenger's seat.

in this one
i start telling the truth

      but it sure
          does
            take
            awhile.

echo.

i found my mother's baby name list once
the name i ended up with
nowhere accounted for
instead
penciled in a leaning line
easter
blue
i guess that's what you get
growing up in california
wolf
tacey
echo
bigger names than i could ever account for
for a kid afraid of everything else
i didn't grow up afraid of the dark
more afraid of the recognition
of myself in the dark
knew myself in the word
cavern
found
what i was made of
                    of the cavern within me
            being bigger than any cavern i would ever find myself in
                    of the vastness of who i was
            always reaching terrifyingly beyond what i could see
it all came down to what one could bear
but i hadn't recognized any breaking points yet
only more cavern
so i kept salting
kept boiling
kept swallowing
on the way to being
which was only ever really code for doing
since i only ever really did things
rather than became them
when there was too much of me to ever really become
i came back to square one every time

                    squarely stuck between
            born on a fault line
clinging to those edges
whiteknuckle afraid to fall moorless into the infinite middle
sisyphus and i rolled that rock up the hill but i never made it to the top
not once
always stopped at the mouth of my own cave
kept every boulder
to keep anything from coming in
                            or out of that darkness i knew could not be good
and we stayed like that for years
all my mouths and me
shut against secrets
(but
of course
that meant shut against
everything else too
but who's counting when there's a cave—that could not be good—to get lost in)

i sang myself canary every time
introduced myself at parties as
just some small thing
wrote my name on every page as
little bird
promised
i was only
feather and yellow
only singing the sweet notes
swore
there's no coal here
no mine
only sweet
only soft

the canaries
go first
our lives
are up for grabs

i avoid any sound from within
for years
cringe at any whisper
any proof of that cave
swallow boulder
after boulder
after boulder
cram myself full of stone
and salt
and still
i know it's there
waiting
indefinite and dark
echo
the name they meant to use
the thing i always was

the echo was me
and mine
the voice whispering back through the dark
was my own
and what i fed it
it fed me
my heart had called itself canary
but i was more than my heart
i was the coal mine
all of me
i was all the space inside
talk about real
estate
all i had been afraid of
all this time
it was all only me

here i was
all these years
singing myself canary

when i've been coal mine all along
even when the ghost would not give me up,
i was mine
dark
and vast
with something small and yellow
singing inside.

(still) unpacking the knapsack

before she met my father
my mother loved a man named rodrigo
who gave her a doll from his home in mexico
and lime popsicles
and a ring
and a promise
she could not keep
the same old story:
girl meets boy
girls loves boy
girl's family gets in the way.
you know the one:
she's white,
he's not,
mom and dad refuse,
she cedes,
they end,
the end.
that's the story
the one without which
i would not be here.

to account for myself
is to account for the whiteness
that's the story
that's my story
the seed of it
like the sea that ruins or redeems us
like the tide that turned
and washed out the hope of their union
that's the story
that accounts for their not being,
that accounts for mine.

it has everything
and nothing to do
with me

like whiteness itself
and the story i carry in my skin
and the wrong its done to others
over time and space and system
has everything
and nothing to do
with me
the backdrop upon which every other facet of
myself
is hung
but not fixed
or fixed
but not fact
is reality
but not real
is truth
but not true
a case of story that creates fact
compounded
by fiction
and by faction
and story
counts for more than
it can account for
counts for more than
any data or measure or fact
that might seek to uproot it
now, like always
i both am
and am not
the story
even as i live and die by it
a story so ubiquitous
so hidden in plain sight
so well worn
we have scarcely
sought to imagine
an alternative path
the way i have grown

so used to the manhattan sidewalk
i forget
we are an island
we are
a small thumb of land
surrounded by sea

i look up and see
gulls
white and full breasted
in the blue sky above canal street
we are an island
we are a ship at sea
we are headed somewhere
we have lived
and died
so long
by this broken invention
by this ruinous lullaby
it seems it could not bear
repeating
and yet
here i am
needing to repeat it:
we must imagine a new map
that will account for all of us
and tell whole stories
by our steering

strangers on a train.

the man across from me
sleeps softly on the c train

someone loves him
i remember
there is someone he's hurt
      someone he's lost
      something he's failed at
            forgotten
            quit
            begun again

and
more often than not
in the overwhelm
i forget we two are each—
waking and sleeping—
every bit as human
though i will never hear
a single thought of his
likely never know his name
more likely still
never lay eyes on him again
and still
what could be more true
a human experience
than this
than waking and resting
and watching
and thinking
together and not
alone and not
sharing
and
not
as we wind through the
veins of the city

the millions of pages
of this great
inevitable book
      stories swallowed
      and lives yet unlived

we come out up over the east river
i watch the light spread over my skin
a distance that could
and could not
be crossed
there was someone else's life there
under my nails
after all this clawing
i see this and know
i know less now
than i have ever known
which was maybe just growing up
or growing out
          down
              and sideways
                  and around
                      in all directions
my compass spinning
the wheels screech as we hit
a bend in the tracks
but this path
was ours
was mine
and we could not
i could not
fall off
with quiet irreverence
i inch toward understanding
on my knees

i buy a plane ticket
i skip dinner
i swallow the empty space where my pride once was

i try to form words
around what i know:
things hurt
but the grass is still green
the pansies still turn their faces up to the light
even in the grey
even in the space where the sun should be
things hurt
but my legs are still under me
my arms are still strong enough
to hold me

i once saw an episode of a hospital soap opera
where some kid had jumped into
you guessed it
quick-drying cement
as a lovesick stunt
doctors flock in around him
chipping him out
piece by piece
like some living fossil
and as they get to the end
the last piece
the heavy one sitting square in the center of his chest
he turns to the den mother doctor and says,
this is it
the worst is over
and she lets him have it:
that his skin has been leeching poison
of this prison
that *this last piece is heavy*
but it's protecting you from all that poison
running straight to your center
stopping your heart
she lets him have it
you can survive this
but the worst
has not yet come

to myself
to the man on the c train
to orpheus and his long walk back
in equal parts:
you have dug yourself out
you are out here
blinking in the sunlight
you are breathing
and you are not done

i go back to the list
of what i do know
      even if its less now than ever
i follow the map of my vertebrae
to fill the stop gap of my throat with sunlight
to follow forth each ribbon of rib to its point of joining
to lay rest each shoulder shrug should
to unburden the grit of my teeth
to forgive the canyon of each doubt
to hold each threadbare fear up to the light,
      to chart how they are changed when they are faced
to run home the highway of my blood
beating in my ears
        here,
           here,
             here

what else is there to know but
what i can see on the map
in block red letters
just before the doors shut
against the platform
for a moment
for a flash:
     you
        are
           here.

on.

time moved on more elegantly
than i'd have liked
its wheels greased with surprising iniquity
i wanted the floor boards to buckle
the breaks to spit sparks in their vigor
but everything swam by

my brother and i drive a yard at a time
crawling forward over the rain-darkened gravel
eyes like saucers
peeled for the sight of salamanders
in their mysterious, perilous pilgrimage
not knowing the danger rolling overhead
       not salamanders, actually
       newts
       if i'm precise
       which i sometimes am
soaked to the bone
lap full of lizards
tiny hands and feet
kissing the insides of my elbow,
up and down the backs of my hands
so many small things
are just as hard
to hold

and yet even in the dark
i can see them
the poppies are blooming in california
the hills alive with fire
and it is hard for this heart to stay broken

stay
in the not knowing with me
       i want to say
       at first to you
       but more

as always
to myself
don't fall for falling
don't feel for proof
        (where there need not
        can not be any)
orpheus, do not look back
there is more to see here than your closed eyelids can offer
this dark is more worth its salt
        pillar or shaker or else
eurydice told me so
shoot straight
you can see the foot in front of you
and
when you drive in to it
you will see the foot in front of that
and that is enough.

things are not as simple
as the path the crow flies
above from one want to the next
we are winding
and unkempt
but so little survives
asphalt
        or salt, to be sure

just think of what we can be here
in the dirt.

still

the word hung in the air like a comma
like a crack in the door
a chink in armor

still

there was a line on the ceiling
i told time by the shadows moving across it
it rained inside that year

still

i was under
        couldn't help
        and didn't fight
the spell
there was something i wanted
from the sadness
but i did not yet know what

still

it is 2 am and the shadows are not moving.
it is 2 am and i am scratching away at nonsense
wading through the easy bits
trying to say only the things i mean

still

it is still 2 am
time spread
it was viscous
or maybe i was
spreading between each second
pooled out
the clock stretching
dalì like

like the air had expanded between the minutes
and me

still

something i am still trying to be

still
all that possibility
still
all these questions
still
all that promise

still
i am not
and never have been
still
and
still
here
i
am

in another life

one i am not quite living
i can hear
      and understand
           all of the whispers of the world around me.
i heed the wisdom of the honeybee, the river.

      do not hold on so tightly
           said the sea, all feather and salt
                a great bird.

      begin again
           spoke the sun with a voice like a bell
                everywhere at once.

and still
i waited for the moon.
i wait
and every day
she is quiet.

i walk with the great drum of the earth.
i listen to her song.

i whistle with the thistle
i rise with the rose

and still the moon says nothing.

i am flint and ash
i rise again and again
i am lost and found over and over.
i ask questions with every part of me.

finally,

       think about what you love most
               she says
                    more silver than every coin

                    in every palm
                    than every ring
                        on every finger.

       ask the inside of your inside,
       consult your marrow.

       what do you beat against yourself?
       for what do you make yourself a door?
                    she asks, spoon and fiddle and pearl.

       follow that ache.

i listened for the Everything in me.

and Everything said: go home.

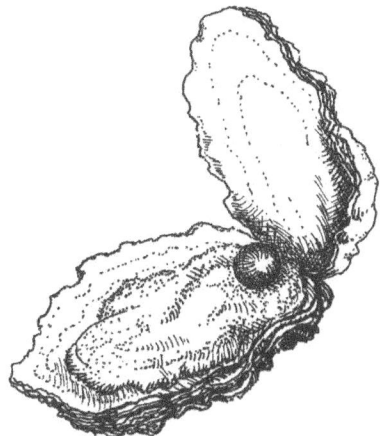

Corey Ruzicano (she/her/hers) is a writer and educator from the San Francisco Bay Area. Whether writing, producing, teaching or riding the subway she seeks to empower voices and stories that encourage empathy. As a creative producer she has worked with P Carl and David Dower at Arts Emerson, Jeanine Tesori at New York City Center and Siena Music, Diana Oh, Victor Cervantes Jr. and Lloyd Suh at Rattlestick Playwrights Theater and The Lark. As a writer her poetry and arts journalism can be found on HowlRound, *Stage & Candor* where she was Editor in Chief and in countless poetry journals. As an educator she has run programs that use arts to teach leadership and emotional intelligence for 826NYC, A BroaderWay, Subway Moon, Second Stage, The National High School Institute, Everytown for Gun Safety, Words on White, and her collective, C.Lab, where she builds programs for non-profits, corporations, schools, and community centers that make spaces for difficult conversations. She assists Claudia Rankine, poet, playwright and Yale University professor and founder of the Racial Imaginary. With all her work, she believes expression belongs to all of us and is necessary to evolution.

www.ingramcontent.com/pod-product-compliance
Lightning Source LLC
Chambersburg PA
CBHW021157090426
42740CB00008B/1125